Master Your Inner Critic

Christopher R. Salem

Published by
Hybrid Global Publishing
355 Lexington Avenue
New York, NY 10017

Manufactured in the United States of America, or in
the United Kingdom when distributed elsewhere.

Salem, Christopher
Master Your Inner Critic
Resolve the Root Cause Create Prosperity

Paperback: 978-1-938015-52-6
eBook: 978-1-938015-53-3

Cover design by: Joe Potter

www.christophersalem.com

Table of Contents

Foreword

If you have opened this book, you are someone who wants to succeed. Perhaps you're seeking financial freedom; or career satisfaction; or a deeply fulfilling relationship. Maybe you want to write a best seller; or run a marathon; or sail across an ocean. Or maybe you just want to find a date; or lose some weight; or reclaim some joy.

You've tried; God knows you've tried. Sometimes you've even had a glimmer of hope; you've seen some progress. Then all of a sudden, you've slid back to where you began. Or worse.

But no matter how hard you work to achieve success, something always seems to be getting in your way. Time passes; and you never get any closer to you goals.

Well luckily, you're in the right place. This small, but powerful, book will finally help you bust through what's been holding you back. The life you want will be yours.

With this book, you will—once and for all—decipher the code; you will unlock the secret

Because, you see, a lot of folks see success as something of a mystery, a black box. They see it as something that happens by chance; something that's reserved for a lucky few; something set aside for the 1%.

But, that's not true. Success is like a cake recipe. When you follow the recipe, you will succeed. There are proven success principles and strategies and tools that when you use and apply them, they will deliver predictable and reliable results.

I learned this the hard way. When I first started my law firm decades ago, I was winging it. I had no clue. I had no clue how to advertise or market or have sales conversations. I had no idea how to do business development or land clients . . . let alone how to actually do the work! I had no clue as to what actually yielded results and what didn't.

I was good at throwing money at stuff . . . but pretty randomly. I'd chase the latest Yellow Page promotional schemes (that's dating myself I know), and then later lead generation gigs, and then Internet pay per click advertisements. SEO and SEM and S & M . . . just checking to see if you're still reading. . . .

I was successful. But by accident; not by design. And not without wasting a lot of time and money. And not without a lot of stress. Because the success wasn't linear. There were these huge ups and downs. The entrepreneurial roller coaster as Darren Hardy might say. No predictability that I could rely on. Up and down. Feast or famine.

Because I had no system; no recipe.

That's, of course, how I stumbled into my coaching and consulting biz. Haphazardly. Without a plan. Without a system. Without a recipe. And when you do (or don't do!) the same thing, you tend to get the same results. Haphazard. Inconsistent. Unreliable.

But, at that juncture, I couldn't afford haphazard. Too much was at stake. I had a lawyer's income that I had relied on, that my family had relied on. There were mortgages and bills and overhead and infrastructure. I didn't have the luxury of 'doing what I loved' hoping that the money would follow. (Hope is not a strategy as I tell my clients.) I didn't want the risk. I couldn't have the risk.

So after stumbling around in the darkness . . . and experiencing way too much uncertainty (you may read this as way too many really lean months with bills that were late, and credit card companies that were calling, and college tuitions that were due), I sought out a system. And found one.

From time to time, I got tempted to go rogue . . . to try out my own entrepreneurial ideas. And then I stopped myself short. Somebody had taken the time to engineer a system . . . to write out a recipe. I better follow the recipe, I thought. And I did.

And it worked. Together with my beautiful business partner (and life partner) Ann Sheybani, I created a way to do the work in the world that I cared about deeply . . . serving talented entrepreneurs and business professionals all around the world . . . coaching, collaborating, creating . . . writing, speaking, sharing . . . with the freedom to travel and adventure all around the globe . . . with the ability to spend much of our year on a beautiful hillside overlooking the North Atlantic in County Cork, Ireland, with a prosperity and joy we could once only dimly hope for.

Because I followed a recipe.

Sometimes, when I'm coaching a client who is just starting out in business, I'll see them trying to deviate from the recipe . . . wanting to go off piste like I once did . . . wanting to do it their own way. Of course it usually doesn't yield the results they imagine.

Chris Salem has created a powerful recipe here. Follow it.

Here's another thing I know for sure: Mindset matters. Will power matters. How we set our mind, how we think, actually affects outcome.

In their book, Mindset: The New Psychology of Success, Stanford professors Greg Walton and Carol Dweck establish convincingly that those who believe in the strength of will are far more likely to overcome life's challenges than those who believe that will power is a limited and exhaustible resource.

We actually have the capacity to will our way to success. If we believe we can, we much more likely will.

Now, of course, this is not exactly *new*.

Will has been around since man first roamed the Garden of Eden.

In every moment, we get to exercise our will. In every moment, we get to choose.

We can choose to be angry at the telemarketer; or grateful that we have a phone. We can choose to be frustrated by the line at the register; or grateful that we have the resources to shop. We can choose to be depressed about the economy; or grateful that we live in a free society.

To be sure, the exercise of will is not always easy.

I know this all too well: going out the door on a dark morning run in the rain; or going to the gym on a cold winter's afternoon; or when I face an unpleasant battle in the courtroom.

I know too from my experiences in mountaineering and distance running that my body has the capacity to push far beyond what my mind thinks it's capable of; that a failure of will is far more likely than a failure of strength.

Viktor Frankl in his shattering death camp memoir, *Man's Search For Meaning*, reminds us, though, that even in the most desperate of circumstances, we have the power to choose how we will be.

Happiness is a choice, says author Gretchen Rubin. And preacher Joel Osteen reminds us of our capacity—and our obligation—each day—to choose joy.

The exercise of will—our power to choose—is our greatest gift.

But there is an evil force at work that gets in your way of choosing the path to prosperity, that keeps you from finally following through on that recipe for success: what I call "your head trash."

For nearly three decades, a dear friend of mine was a flight attendant on a major airline flying long-haul routes. He tells this funny story: At the end of an especially long, customer service-challenged flight, when they would come down the aisle for that last time with the garbage bags, saying "your trash, your trash," what they were really thinking (and actually saying), was "you're trash, you're trash!"

Yes, amusing. But the reality is that every single one of us is carrying around some trash . . . in our heads.

Your head trash—your inner critic as Chris calls it—is what keeps you stuck; it's what keeps you from launching your business, writing your book, advancing your career, getting in shape, finding a mate, speaking your truth; it's what keeps you from sharing your gifts with the world; it's what keeps you from living your very best life.

Your head trash is comprised of those voices in your head that whisper to you:

- I'm not ready

- I'm not enough

- I'm not worthy

- I need more training

- I need more experience

- I need a degree

- I need another certification

And *no one* escapes those voices.

Tony Robbins suggests that the two primary questions that every human being struggles with are: "Am I enough?" and "Will I be loved?"

Brené Brown, in her beautiful book, *The Gifts of Imperfection*, says that every single one of us comes face to face with self-doubt; that every single one of us questions our worth; that no one escapes that worry that someone will find out that we are a fraud.

So . . . recognizing that you're not that "special," that you're not alone, that every single one of us struggles; every single one of us confronts these fears and doubts . . . the only relevant question then is this: What are you going to do *now*?

Even in the face of fear and doubt: What action will you take? What commitment will you make?

Chris and I both know from decades of coaching experience that strategies and tools are easy to teach.

Mindset, though, is what really matters.

Silence the negative voices of your inner critic. Get rid of your head trash.

Dive right in here. Don't wait.

The clock is ticking; and the world needs you.

Step up. Step out. Get busy. Start now.

Follow Chris Salem's wise words. Your dreams await you.

Walt Hampton, J.D.
Best Selling Author of *Journeys on the Edge:
Living a Life That Matters* and President of
Book Yourself Solid® Worldwide
Castletownshend, Co. Cork, Ireland
September 2016

Introduction

What Can This Book Do for You?

The solutions presented in this book come from my own personal experience and those of countless people I have mentored and coached over the years. It comes from the heart and truly addresses the source where the problem lies so you can release it and move forward toward your greatness. The mission of this book is to empower people to come out of their comfort zones and use their Inner Critic in a positive way to manifest the life they desire in their business and personal lives. But it's not saying that this is the only way or should resonate with everyone. What you perceive is up to you, whether or not you agree with the message and solutions presented here.

I wrote this book for those who currently are struggling in their careers, personal relationships, family life, or any combination thereof. Business and personal life make up the majority of our lives—this is where we spend our time and derive meaning. The goal of this content is not to merely creating awareness but truly connecting people with solutions that address the root cause that creates the effects that hold us back. Please note, you can have more than one effects, but they often stem from one root cause. Our society in general focuses on managing or servicing the effects we live with each day and does not address the root cause or problem. In this book, I've used actual examples and stories to further connect with you with the solutions that can improve the quality of your life.

The struggle we experience resonates inside of us. It's our very own Inner Critic. The messages, often subliminal, play over and over in our heads like an old tape, dictating how we act, talk, and interact with others. These messages can be both positive and negative, but most of us typically tend to gravitate toward the negative. Often those negative messages tell us that we are the enemy; this usually is triggered from past unpleasant events that continue to play out in our career, relationships, and families. The negative side of the Inner Critic, if not dealt with properly, can lead to habits and behaviors that do not serve us, such as addiction (drugs, alcohol, gambling, sex, food) and negative emotions stemming from anger, guilt, and shame. When these habits and behaviors escalate, they can lead to self-sabotage and even death. The aftermath also affects other close to you like family, friends, and co-workers.

The good news is that you are not alone. You do not have to be held prisoner to your Inner Critic. You have a choice, and it all starts with awareness about where you are now. Understanding and addressing the root cause is central toward resolving the issues that prevent you from becoming your better self and rob you of success. Use the content in this book to silence the negative messages of your inner critic and reclaim the joy, happiness, and success you deserve. Remember, you have a choice, and no one is can do it for you. Now is the time to make it happen. Make a pact with yourself that if the content shared here resonates with your core, you will take the action steps presented to change the quality of your life and no longer allow your inner critic to keep you stuck in habits and behaviors that do not serve you in a healthy and productive way.

To your health and prosperity,
Christopher R. Salem
Prosperneur™

Confront and Release the Devil Inside

"There is nothing either good or bad, but thinking makes it so."

William Shakespeare

Have you asked yourself from time to time why your life has not unfolded the way you have envisioned? What holds you back from accomplishing your goals and achieving success? The answer is hidden in past childhood events: the root cause that leads to current negative effects in your life. Like many people, you live in the effects, and this keeps you trapped in self-doubt, procrastination, and other habits that do not serve you. Now that you are an adult, your habits and behaviors are unconsciously linked to events that have molded you into a pattern of either self-doubt (your inner critic) or success (your best self). Your inner critic dictates the habits and behaviors that do not serve you long term.

Let's take a look at various effects and their root causes:

- Effect: Low self-esteem, low self-confidence
  Cause: Overbearing parent, or being bullied as a child or teenager

- Effect: Procrastination
  Cause: Lack of desire, not knowing your "why" in life

- Effect: Lack of wealth
  Cause: Focus on lack, being taught you don't deserve to prosper

- Effect: Not advancing in your career
  Cause: Being taught as a child that you aren't good enough

- Effect: Emotional eating
  Cause: Viewing food as comfort to mask negative emotion

- Effect: Sense of unworthiness
  Cause: Lack of attention from parent or family during childhood

Many people work on their problems by addressing the effects rather than the root cause. People who lack confidence often use positive self-talk and go through the motions without fully understanding first *why* they lack confidence. Positive self-talk without first addressing the root cause is an external action that only provides a temporary, perceived state of confidence—not a long-term solution.

Another example is procrastination. People try continuously (with miserable results) to use self-discipline to address procrastination instead of looking at what is causing it and why. This may offset procrastination slightly for the moment, but the results will always come up short. Without addressing the cause, discipline alone is not successful; it's only a matter of time before procrastination returns.

People gravitate to get-rich-quick ideas rather than understand why they are experiencing a lack of wealth in the first place. If someone does come into wealth but does not possess a mindset of prosperity, the chances of retaining it is unlikely. He or she will often spend it or mishandle money and revert back to same state of worth.

So why do we focus our efforts on the effects of our problems? The answer is that effects are consciously observable, making it easy to address them. People see immediate progress toward their goals, but in reality this is a false perception. Addressing the root cause is scary, difficult, and very complicated; thus most people run for the door when they realize the real issues are beneath the surface. Many of us do not know how to go about uncovering the true cause in the first place. So when we focus on the problem via effects, the results are marginal at best.

For example, take a man who has never been able to live up to his full potential with his career. He may have had a father that was overbearing and always on him to improve his performance or skills. He may have also felt neglected because his father was never there for important events or did not acknowledge him for his successes growing up. These are trigger events that develop the root cause that eventually leads to effects in adulthood that will mold self-defeating habits and behaviors. Living in the effect will not change his current situation because he's operating from self-doubt. His Inner Critic defaults to the negative (by choice of course, as there is always a choice between the positive and negative) and unconsciously feeds off the root cause that creates habits and behaviors that do not serve him. He has lived his entire life not being his authentic-self; instead he has always tried to be someone his dad or other authoritative figures wanted him to be in life. Does this sound like someone you know? Does it perhaps sound like you?

Another example is a man who struggles with being overweight and cannot seem to gain respect from women in his life. His career is stagnant, never advancing from a tactical position. He had a relatively decent upbringing, with no traumatic events. However, his mother, who was slightly domineering, would often require him to eat everything on his plate, telling him that good food is expensive and others in third-world countries were not as fortunate. His mother, while not intending to be malicious, planted a seed of guilt her young son.

In addition to not losing weight despite using several weight-release programs, this man also gravitated to women who were more dominant than him. It was the same with his career; he always had a subservient role and didn't take advantage of opportunities to advance as a leader. Can you see the pattern here?

He was not conscious of this underlying cause and during coaching did not recognize this at first. It was only through consistent questions that we were able to identify his root cause. Once he acknowledged this, he was able to truly forgive his mother—and most importantly, himself—and then fully release it. In time he was able to adopt healthier and more productive habits. His new mind-set allowed him to lose weight and keep it off, choose a woman who was not dominant (but also not submissive), and finally break out of his comfort zone to take on new challenges in order to grow in his career as a leader.

My own story is somewhat similar to the first example; as a young boy, I longed for approval from my father and wanted to be recognized for my successes in school and sports. However, my father was not there during those critical years when I was growing up. The cause in my case was the void or neglect created by not having my father present during those important years when father-and-son bonding is critical for the healthy development of confidence and mind-set. As a child, I was aware on some level that my dad was busy working, but on another level the reality of his neglect hurt me to the core.

Growing up I was skilled at sports and had average grades in school, but I always questioned these skills. I saw myself as not good enough and required approval from authoritative figures such as coaches and teachers. This self-doubt and lack of confidence escalated during puberty through my early adult years, when my life operated from a negative emotion we know as anger. The emotion of anger fueled my life which led to a high-like feeling (similar to being on drugs) and manifested itself in rebellious behaviors that were self-destructive, such as vandalism, binges and overuse of drugs and alcohol (which were nearly fatal twice), and a sexual addiction so powerful that it masked the pain and self-doubt I lived with every day. It gave me a sense of bravado that I projected out to the world, which fooled many people.

No matter what I did, even if it was good or I excelled at something, it still was not good enough in my eyes! The quest for approval from my father unconsciously was the cause that created the effects that led to behaviors that masked the problem and did not serve me long-term. Years later I came to understand that my father experienced the same things I did; he lived his short life with the same pain, masking it with similar addictive behaviors. His goal was success, which he achieved, but it meant sacrificing his family in the process. However, he never addressed the root cause of all his pain, and so it affected him his entire life, just as my pain was doing to me. He made an attempt at the end to recoup the time lost, but his life was cut short from cancer. He fulfilled his goal to be successful but the regret of sacrificing his family manifested itself into illness that unfortunately took him out of this world far too soon at fifty-six years old.

I highly admire my father for his work ethic, which I inherited, and I fully understood during my personal transformation years ago that what he did was not personal to me but only what he knew at the time. It was part of my healing process to know that it was my responsibility to either hold onto the pain or release it. Living in denial and always trying to manage the effects in my life got me nowhere. It was exhausting going through the motions each day; even though I was financially successful during that time, I was emotionally bankrupt. As I felt waves of anger spewing from me like an eruption from a volcano, the release was powerful. This negative energy had taken hostage of my well-being and had never allowed me to enjoy the true feeling of success in my career, family, and personal life. Releasing it was like an albatross that fell from my neck, and over the next few months I began to feel more comfortable in my own skin for the first time.

The old saying goes, "Nothing changes until you change." It is a choice to live in the effect or address the cause, and then fully release it from your core and inner essence. Now there is living in the past or dwelling too far into the future. Instead it's being who you are right now in the present and molding new habits that move you toward a transformation of a better self. This will ultimately impact people around you in a positive way and begin to attract better situations and opportunities for more success in your career, family, and personal relationships.

Can someone who is stuck in life—whether in their career, personal life, or both—change and move toward success? Can such person operate from a place of peace without anxiety? The answer is YES, but only when you start addressing the root cause in your life. Your life is an evolving story and can change when you choose to change for the better. Your life is not confined by past events that negatively affected you; they can be used to strengthen what you can become in a positive way. The journey to eliminate self-doubt begins with addressing the root cause.

So, how do you identify and release the root cause fully and begin to live a productive and healthy life in the moment? Let's examine the process below.

Finding the root cause that creates multiple causes that create the effects is vitally important for true change to take place. Please note, there can be more than one cause that leads to multiple effects that all stem from the root cause. See the flow chart above to see how this can be analyzed to get to your root cause.

Remember, the key goal is uncovering the root cause, not just the various causes that lead to effects. True change cannot occur without fully addressing the root cause. This can prove to be very difficult for people since it involves digging deep into the problem, and for some, into the subconscious mind. The more aware you are and the higher your consciousness, the more likely you will be to trace each cause back to the origin.

It's very common to conclude that a particular cause is the root cause, especially if you're not clear on what makes up the entire spectrum of effects and causes. Sometimes you may simply run into a dead-end because you can't think of any preceding cause. The best thing to do is to try and dig as much as you can and identify the most fundamental cause; this will probably be sufficient to effect sizable change in your situation. Over time, as you increase your consciousness, the other causes will become clearer to you. Let's examine below how you can find your secondary causes along with the root cause.

- **Take moral inventory of yourself.** Just as in the 12-Step program, go back and write down any issues even you perceive them not to really bother you! This is very important and should not be taken for granted. Write down everything again, even if it does not seem to be a perceived trigger event or issue. Often people do not realize that certain events that happened long ago have affected their lives and play out every day in what they do that does not serve them.

- **Recognize that the root cause always lies inside you.** It is tied back to your past experiences, choices, behaviors, and beliefs. Go deep and you will discover where the problem lies.

- **Confront the root cause by looking truthfully at yourself.** Look at yourself in the mirror and accept responsibility. Appreciate this negative experience if you created it. Acknowledge the cause even if you did not create it but were a victim of this circumstance. Forgive the person(s) who hurt you. You do not have to forget, but just truly forgive. Forgiving is vital, and you will know it is being released when you feel waves of various emotions being flushed out of your body. You may feel lighter and begin to have a clear mind soon after as a result of releasing the cause. This may take several times to complete—you may not truly release it the first time. It takes strength and a firm commitment to truly release it. You will feel like a weight has been lifted from your body once it is truly released. Let it go either way, as the story of your life is always evolving and is not defined only by these causes from trigger events. This can be scary, but it is the only way to release the cause that creates the effects that no longer serve you. You can also do this with a therapist, coach, or an unbiased friend. Use them to build your strength in a positive way and continue to develop a story that operates from a place of joy, happiness, and peace rather than negative emotions such as anger, shame, and guilt.

- **Find the common denominator of the causes that stem from the root cause.** Carefully go back and thoroughly analyze them. What is the common denominator across these causes? Go deep; you may not get to the root cause at first, but you will find the key link to it. Always trust your gut feeling and go with it.

- **Practice increasing your self-awareness.** Just like anything you practice, you will become attuned to things you were not previously aware of before. The higher your self-awareness, the more likely you will be able to identify the cause and effect that leads to the root cause.

When you release the root cause and truly let it go, it will unlock the feeling of true peace and joy. You will know that your life is about choices, and when you come from your authentic self, your story will lead you to success over time. Coming from joy and peace, your decisions to act promptly rather than procrastinate will be easier and the fear of failure will be less. You will have more confidence that your abilities are coming from your authentic self, and you will know that the universe will play its part if you play yours with 100 percent commitment and action. You will know that fear is just fear itself, not tied to an actual objective or goal you have planned. You will know that success is a journey, not a destination, and the only true failure in life is not starting, confronting, or following through on something you fear. Always know that fear is an illusion. It is not real, but only appears so when you focus and give energy to it.

Questions to Ask Your Inner Critic

How do you feel in the current moment?

What is not working right in your life?

Why do you do what you do right now?

What trigger events in the past cause you to feel the way you do? (Remember, it can be more than one. Be honest with yourself. List them all and be specific along with what you truly feel with each one.)

What is the common denominator with the cause(s) that creates the struggle in your life?

What is your root cause?

It is important you address these questions honestly with yourself and don't answer from someone else's perspective. Come from your heart even if the truth hurts, and be specific with your answers. Remember, your reality cannot shift toward the direction you desire without properly addressing your root cause and moving forward to embrace change. I did this almost twenty years ago, and you can do it, too. There is nothing different about me or other successful people compared to you. It's just the ability to create a life you deserve by removing the bottlenecks. It's similar to examining a business by looking at each business unit. It all comes down to the root cause. Find it and then eliminate it and move toward your excellence.

Embrace Change

"Your life does not get better by chance; it gets better by change."

Jim Rohn

Releasing the root cause that binds you is often the most difficult step as you begin mastering your inner critic. However, it does not end there; it requires a process over time to fully develop your Inner Critic to work for you in all areas of your life. The next step to mastering your inner critic is the process of embracing change. It must be clear to you from the start that making a conscious choice to achieve more success in your life must be embraced as a journey, not a destination.

Change is constant and happens around us all the time. So why do we resist it or fear it? The answer is that many of us are comfortably being uncomfortable even if things in our life are stagnant. Often, it takes an unforeseen situation, such as the loss of a job or relationship, to take us out of our comfort zone. When you release the root cause, this is a breakthrough period, but you must embrace change in order to master your inner critic or create the life you desire. You have to come out of your comfort zone, not just once but often on an ongoing basis. Jim Rohn famously expressed how what you become in the process of change is valuable to your growth. Being open-minded and following your purpose—your "Why"—is the next step to creating a better way in your career and relationships.

Eastern philosophy teaches that nothing in life is permanent and everything can change on a dime. When you adopt the mind-set of embracing change, you are then better able to enjoy the journey despite the obstacles along the way. Struggle occurs when you resist change, so it is always better to embrace and follow your true purpose rather than resist it. Resisting change creates emotions such as anxiety, anger, guilt, and shame. These emotions are part of living in the effects that we covered in Step 1. When you release the root cause and make the commitment to embrace change, there is no going back to living in the effects of your life. It always works out in the end— there is always a light at the end of tunnel—but you have to be patient with the process. Welcome the new and release the past with gratitude.

Change is necessary to move toward mastering your inner critic, but there is always a choice of how to look at things during the experience. It comes down to your perception, whether positive or negative. One suggestion is to alter your perspective by attaching positive labels to your feelings during the process. For example, you may experience uneasiness in your stomach, which can be perceived as anxiety. Look at this not from experiencing anxiety (which is negative), but instead as a temporary feeling of discomfort (which is positive) that something valuable will result from change. The key is to focus on the positive and direct that energy toward the feeling of joy that will attract the results you desire. Take a deep breath and know that embracing change is the answer to fulfilling your purpose. Resisting the process has no place here; simply trust that this journey, no matter how scary it may be at first, will lead to more joy and meaning in your life.

Embracing change is something I used to find very difficult to grasp. From the time I was eight years old all the way through high school, I hoped my father would show up at some of my ball games. My father was also very competitive with me during my teen years into early adulthood. His way was to pay for something that would address my need but not allow me to work for it. When I worked for something, it would make him feel uneasy and give him the sense of losing control. The inability to acknowledge and accept this led to anger issues throughout my teen years into early adulthood. As I mentioned in Step 1, since I refused to acknowledge and accept this change, it led to me to live in the effect that created the chronic emotion of anger. Living in the effect provided me with great energy to succeed on some level across various areas of my life into early adulthood, but it also prevented me from advancing to a higher level of success.

This undoing created friction with others and manifested itself in situations and experiences of being letdown, which only further fueled my anger. This anger in some way gave me a high, as though it were a drug. For example, when I was thirty years old, I was hired by a trade show company to launch two events from scratch. In my previous company I had a reputation for launching successful trade events. In the new company, my senior manager was much older than me. At first he was very friendly, sports-minded like me, and success-oriented. Subconsciously on some level he was the father figure I had longed for throughout my childhood.

My goal was to accomplish the task of launching two shows from scratch, and I was determined to make that happen, no matter what. However, the environment

I worked in was not healthy. Many people gossiped, talked behind each other's backs, and were threatened by hard work. They would huddle at certain people's desks to talk about others negatively and would meet in the cafeteria to do the same. Soon I found out that my boss was often being the ringleader of these gossip discussions. Even though I was an angry man, it was not my style to talk negatively about others and waste energy that way. I grew tired of these discussions and began to eat my lunch outside of this circle. In addition, my father was dying of lung cancer, and I would often spend the little time I had at lunch to check on him.

My manager was insulted when I stopped having lunch with him and my coworkers daily. But I considered this negative talk toxic and detrimental to keeping the momentum going toward building these two new trade events, and I was also struggling with losing my father slowly to cancer at such a young age. He also began to make things difficult for me by pulling certain resources which then made it difficult to see these two events to fruition. He was very abrupt with me, and over time many of his comments became personal. He was insulted that I didn't attend his Christmas party due to needing to be with my father, who died four days later.

Over a six-month period, I was still able to launch the events from scratch with limited resources, even though launching such events usually took twelve to eighteen months. However, the unthinkable happened two days before the launch of first of the events. The senior manager let me go without any explanation. When I went to confront him, he was nowhere to be found. Many of the companies I had sold were in shock and did not understand why I was not there. They were told that I had left the company on my own. The good news was that these two events went on to be successful and were later sold to another company a year later.

What is the lesson here? It's that living in the effect that fueled the emotion of anger that drove me created this situation. Subconsciously at the time, I initially viewed the person I worked for as the father figure I never had while growing up, but I soon discovered he was actually very similar to my father. He was competitive, controlling, and could not tolerate someone who refused to be controlled. I had manifested this situation because I was living in the effect from certain causes rather than addressing the root cause firsthand. In addition, I had refused to embrace the change necessary to address my problems, but instead masked them with my addictions. It was at this time that I had a spiritual awakening—and it's so ironic that it happened so soon after my father's passing. I knew I had to stop living in the effect of certain causes (anger) and begin to address the root cause. A

12-Step program gave me the skills to take a moral inventory and begin the journey toward truly letting go and striving for real success in life. I learned what it meant to be authentic and connect with my "Why," thus creating a life that offered value to others. Below are a few steps I used to embrace change and connect to my "Why" and the life I desired, both in business and personally.

1. **Acknowledge and accept change.**

   Change in life happens in life whether you like it not. The key is to stop resisting and go with the flow, and then learn from these experiences to move toward what works best for you. Stop being in denial; when you are in the flow, you have the control to change things you can and let go freely of what you cannot control. I am not religious, but I strongly believe in the energy of the Universe. The serenity prayer is so helpful in any situation: "God, grant me the serenity to accept the things I cannot change, courage to change the things I can, and wisdom to know the difference."

2. **Find the meaning in each experience and learn from it.**

   When you truly let go and release the root cause, you begin to shift your mind toward higher planes of consciousness or self-awareness. Look for meaning in each experience of change, whether positive or negative. Use what you learn to gravitate toward what you desire to become, and always be in the flow. Being in the flow will also alleviate your fear, which will always try to derail your progress. Know that fear is merely an illusion, and only you have the choice to repel it or being absorbed by it.

3. **Reduce expectations, but not toward your long-term goal.**
   It is fine to have reasonable expectations of how you'd like something to turn out as part of your short-term goals, but always detach yourself from the outcome. Reducing or having no expectations about your business, relationships, or any situation allows you to always be in the flow, have fun, and keep focused on long term goals. When you have higher expectations, you are likely to meet with disappointment. Detaching yourself from the outcome is a must to stay in the flow. Let it be, put your energy toward what you can control, and let go of the rest.

Questions to Ask Your Inner Critic

What do I fear right now when it comes to change?

Why do I have this perception of fear for change in the current moment?

Take a deep breath and state: "My fear is not reality; it is just an illusion." Say this several times while staring at yourself in the mirror, and then say, "I am worthy of a better life, and now that I have let go of the root cause, the possibilities for embracing change are endless." Practice repeating, "I am letting go and going with the flow to truly embrace change." Visualize your

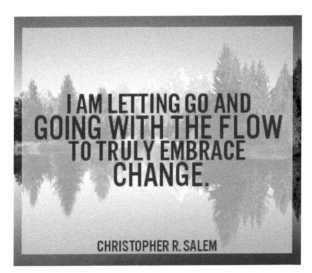

goal, but detach yourself from the outcome for each step of the process on this journey.

Keep it simple and enjoy the process even if you do not feel like it in the beginning. Smile often, even when you do not feel like it, as this will enhance your mood and shift positive thoughts toward embracing change and reducing fear. Focus on the positive even when negative or self-defeating thoughts try to derail you. Positive thoughts followed by action and a true commitment to change will shift positive energy toward embracing change. Obstacles will and do occur, but they are only a test of your true commitment to change. You can do this!

Step into Your Fear

"Everything you want is on the other side of fear."
Jack Canfield

We have been conditioned to think that all fear is real and can threaten our well-being. Why is this the case? Think about it: When you were very young child, if your parents didn't tell you not to cross a busy road alone, you would have done it without fear. This type of fear is legitimate, as crossing a busy road when very young without adult supervision could have a grave impact on your life. Fear is a natural response to physical and emotional danger—if we did not feel it, then we could not protect ourselves from legitimate threats. Fear triggers a "fight or flight" response that prepares us to take action to protect ourselves. This type of fear is good; it plays a positive role to protect us from things that threaten our lives.

However, we are taught at a very young age to fear even situations that are far from life-and-death situations. As we learned in Step 1, trigger events such as negative experiences and trauma in one's life are the root cause that spawns other causes that create the effects we live daily. We live in the effect: What we feel as fear holds us back from a life of peace, prosperity, and success. These personal demons that we fear are not truly life-threatening, but they are perceived that way.

Many fears are based in false beliefs or from trigger events that created the root cause. For example, does fear keep you from advancing in your career because of trigger events that happened in school when you were growing up? You may have been bullied or picked on, and this feeling of humiliation now prevents you from taking advantage of career opportunities that would change the quality of your life. When you advance in your career, it means surrounding yourself with self-confident people that you may perceive as threats to your well-being, because they remind you of the ones in school that hurt you. Playing it safe and listening to fears that in reality does not harm them often lead people to choose being unhappy rather than happy.

As a kid I had a lack of respect for authority, with the exception of a few of my coaches in sports. When faced with situations during my early to late teen years where there was authority, I would rebel or fail to follow the authority figure's lead. It was my perceived fear that these authority figures would draw conclusions about me and reject me or would fail to follow through when I most required their time. This fear was relative or assumed, not absolute. It was not real, but it was an illusion that seemed all too real to me at the time. Obviously it did not threaten my life, but because of my perception, it later led to behaviors that did not serve me or others. Again, these were addictive behaviors that resulted from living in the effects of the root cause.

These behaviors were always the result of anger and deep sadness inside of me. Acting out or engaging in addictive behavior led me to carry out acts of vandalism and destruction (fueled by my anger and sadness) throughout my teen years. It was the same for my brother as well. The difference was that I had the ability to use fear to protect me from situations that truly threatened my life, whereas that was not the case with him. I would jump motorcycles with the use of ramps, but I would think it through before proceeding because I knew it could be life-threatening. My brother, on the other hand, engaged in reckless behavior, not thinking twice about the consequences. His situation led to him almost dying four times; twice he was declared dead before coming back to life.

Everything during those years was a threat to my life even if not truly life-threatening. This further fueled the effects of the root cause I lived in that manifested itself in other unpleasant and negative experiences I created during college and my early adult years. Recreational drug use, alcohol, promiscuous sex, food, and more masked the fear and the effects I lived in during those years. These addictive habits eventually subsided once I got clean and sober. However, the behaviors did not stop until I truly addressed the root cause. It was only then that living in the effects of the time began to disappear and the perceived fear I experienced could be minimized or eliminated when analyzed as not something that posed a physical risk to my well-being. I realized I had a choice to let this negative perceived fear go and commit to action instead.

One of my coaching clients had been verbally and occasionally physically abused by his father as a child. His years as a young adult to around age forty consisted of him resisting authority, be unable to follow direction at work, and not listen effectively to his wife and kids. He was so self-absorbed that his arrogant behavior and self-righteousness eventually pushed away his family and derailed further success in his career, even though he was a business owner. He could not keep employees for long. He perceived all advice or constructive criticism as a personal attack. This was his perceived fear that people in his life, such as employees and even family, had a hidden agenda to harm him. This perceived fear seemed life-threatening on some level. This fear hindered him from developing quality relationships with clients, his employees, and even his wife, who eventually left him. He felt this perceived fear over and over as a result of living in the effects that came from the root cause or other multiple causes.

When you feel fear, always ask yourself if what you fear will truly have dire consequences for your life.

Fear dissipates when you strive for excellence rather than perfection.

Christopher R. Salem

Remember, fear manifests itself through the effects created by the root cause. When you truly release the root cause and embrace change, you can begin to live in the moment, let go, and be in the flow. A relaxed mind-set allows you to consciously analyze fears that are not truly life-threatening. You can then begin to move forward through this perceived fear toward your desired goal, and you'll soon see what you originally perceived as fear has dissipated into the wind. Confronting your fear is a key step to mastering your Inner Critic. Here are some steps you can take to confront your fear.

1) Be Objective and Open-Minded.
Perception determines what we experience in life, whether positive or negative. It is perception that creates the thoughts that lead to how we feel during any given situation. Both thoughts and feelings work together in harmony. However, it should be noted that feelings and thoughts are different from one another—they are not one in the same. Again, thoughts determine how we feel, but how we feel can also alter our thoughts. Feelings are stronger than thoughts; they dictate our action in any given situation.

Let's say, for example, that you are scared to speak in front of an audience. This causes you to feel anxiety or stress, and that influences your actions. It affects your body and how you talk. A feeling of being scared triggers how your body responds when faced with something you fear. The most important thing you can do when confronting fear is to be objective and open-minded to the given situation. Put your emotions aside for the time being and allow yourself to see this situation objectively and recognize what is real and what is delusional. You will often find that the delusional side is what causes the fear. You are then able to see it accurately with a clearer perception without being clouded by emotions or feelings that mask the fear.

Many people dream of owning their own business. It is embedded in their gut; it is at the core of their essence. Many of them express discontent working long hours for someone else in a role that provides no personal satisfaction or joy in their lives. However, some put the fear aside to walk away from a secure job with steady paycheck to pursue their dream, while others allow fear to create the excuses they justify to stay comfortably uncomfortable. Always know that most fear (unless it alerts you to a real risk to your life) can appear rational but in reality is not real. It only becomes real when you give into it and perceive it that way.

When you are truly open-minded and objective, this allows you to honestly look at your dream without fear and decide what works best for you. Making a decision with clear perception is much better than one clouded by emotions due to fear. Know yourself and your strengths and weaknesses, and never overthink or overanalyze a decision to pursue your dream. Again, if that dream plays itself over and over, then it resides in your gut and every fiber in your being is telling you to take a leap of faith, put fear aside, and go after it.

2) Believe in Yourself and Enhance Your Strengths.
Overcoming fear requires you to truly believe in yourself and confidently confront any situation or obstacle on the way to reaching your desired goal. Doubt destroys dreams because it clouds the positive thoughts and feelings you have. For example, it was my dream to pay baseball in the big leagues. While I was a very good player, my physical stature and skills did not align to this level of play beyond college. A proper assessment of this situation would conclude that, while it was a dream at some point in my life, in reality I did not have enough strength and skill to make this work. Taking a risk to pursue this dream would not have been in my best interest. However, my strengths of connecting and empowering others suited me to becoming a coach, which was a much more cal-culated, realistic risk. When your strengths are realis-tic regarding something you desire and you believe in your capabilities, nothing will stand in your way.

3) Detach from the Outcome.
Nothing in life is guaranteed! This is what makes life interesting and worth living. The feeling of success and

living a prosperous life is felt in the journey, not the destination. When the outcome is not guaranteed, this often sways people not to take risks. The perception of fear often stems from the unknown, not knowing whether something will turn out for the best or not. In my years investigating fear, not only within myself but also with others, I have always seen that in the long run everything usually turns out fine—even after the darkest periods. You may not be where you want to be at a given moment, but you can trust that you always have what you require at that time. Sometimes what you want may not in hindsight be what is right for you. There is always a reason, as we will later find out.

I can look back at jobs I had years ago when I was laid off or let go and then fretted about it, consuming so much negative and wasted energy. Later, I realized how grateful I was to have lost those jobs—those experiences led me to become what I am today. The Universe is not predictable but always knows what is best, and we all have to go through some tough times to become what we are meant to be on this journey. This is why detaching oneself from the outcome, letting go and going with the flow, is critical in any given situation.

Confront what you fear. Determine if your strengths are realistic for reaching your desired goal. Give it your best in the present moment, and then let the Universe take care of the rest. Be relaxed and enjoy every step of the process. Your part is to know what you want and then truly visualize the feeling. Truly feeling what one wants is often missed by many people during the visualization process. Make a note to truly feel what you visualize. Words alone will not align with the laws of the Universe; this requires true feelings about what is desired. For example, a person may desire to lead a company at a CEO level, but only feel this at a manager level. People may desire to become millionaires but only feel it as a sense of security, and thus just having enough suffices. Always visualize each feeling in great detail in a positive light, but detach yourself from the outcome. You are responsible for showing up, thinking positively, speaking words that propel you forward, and committing to action. How and when your dream evolves to fruition is up to the Universe. Plant the seed, nurture yourself, and then let things evolve in their own way.

Steps to Address Your Inner Critic

- Begin today practicing acceptance and detachment from your outcome while keeping an open mind. Become aware of when you begin to begin to take control of situations that are out of your control. Practice controlling what is in your control, being open-minded and letting go of what is out of your control. You will feel stress or anxiety when you control something that's out of your control. Conduct this step daily and commit at least ten minutes to becoming aware of this, and then let it go. It will become easier each week with continuous practice.

- Focus on your strengths daily and commit to enhancing them with every opportunity to do so. Become aware when you dwell or begin to put emphasis on things that are your weakness. Delegate to others. Take ten minutes daily at lunch to focus on becoming aware!

Know Your Why

"You gotta have a WHY! You gotta have a reason for why you do what you do!"

Eric Thomas

Your "WHY" defines who you are, what you do, and what drives you. This "why" is embedded in each of us. We all have different passions and strengths, but these are often buried behind the noise in our heads. This is the negative side of your Inner Critic talking to you. Living and working in the effect of your life as a result of the root cause will often prevent you from truly operating from your "why," your true purpose. It is always there, but many have gone through their entire lives and missed out on following their purpose because of ignorance or fear. This was the case with me when I wasn't living a life in alignment with my purpose, but instead was struggling inside, experiencing unhealthy relationships, and not being all I could be in my career. Even though I realized a measure of success due to my drive and work ethic, I felt empty and miserable inside because I was not following my purpose. True success is not measured by how much money you make, but by the value you provide to others and what you become inside. This results in feeling great and having constant joy. This is why it is extremely important before tapping into your "why" that you take the steps to identify and release the root cause that has created the effects you're living in.

You learned in Steps 2 and 3 to embrace change and reduce your fear to a minimum. Without change and facing your fear, it is difficult to get in synch with your true purpose. Remember, it is how you feel inside that creates the words and propels the action to draw from the universal energy in order to manifest your success. It's all about how you feel—this energy is important. Your Inner Critic has two forms of energy: positive and negative. You have the choice to choose which one, and when you take the steps above, it will become easier in time to step into your purpose.

Finding your "why" can be challenging, especially in today's busy word with its multitude of distractions. One way to identify your "why" is to take the time to go to someplace quiet for a few days—perhaps a retreat or a place of solitude. When you are free of distractions and in a calm place, you can begin to go inward and listen to what your inner critic is saying. Remember, it may still tell you things from the negative side, but the key is to let it go and listen closely the positive voice. Let go of everything else, such as your day-to-day obligations, work, family, and other things. Focus on how you feel in that moment and truly listen to what the positive voice tells you.

Write down on paper—not in your phone but *on paper*—what brings you joy and happiness. Write down everything that comes to mind from a place of nonjudgment and not from opinions of others! You will have time later to organize these notes and create a clear vision or plan. Let what you write come from you and be in the flow of that moment. Your why or true purpose should be focused on what makes you happy and feel good, not material things or money, which are by-products of success that should come from your "why." Also, you may discover that you have more than one purpose that drives you. That's okay, too.

Your "why" is the purpose behind the words you speak and the actions you take toward accomplishing your goals. Your purpose, or true calling, has to be clear and well-defined before taking steps to create new relationships and embark on new businesses or entre-preneurship. The reason is that when you encounter potential obstacles along the way, your inner being is not thrown off course since the focus is to always follow your true purpose. You will not be denied in the long run by staying the course. It is like the captain of a ship leading his men to forge ahead toward accomplishing the task at hand despite the elements and obstacles that attempt to derail them. In any personal situation or business, you will be constantly tested, and you have to keep focused in order to succeed. When setbacks occur they will not paralyze you, but instead they will motivate you to go forward and follow your true pur-pose. Having a clearly defined "why" is the foundation of your success.

For several years my perceived "why" was completely distorted. It was based on what I felt would please my father and involved doing something that made money, and lots of it. My work ethic and discipline regarding money was set at a young age, so amassing wealth being in sales came naturally to me. However, the internal struggle I lived every day almost took me out through my addictive behaviors. My "why" did not have a clear focus; it was fueled by the negative emotion called ANGER. It focused on the by-product of success (i.e., money), and who I was back then was not really me—I was trying to be someone I thought my father wanted me to be. I made money, but I had absolutely no joy or happiness.

This was not success in any way. My addictive behaviors masked the root cause, and I lived in the effects of what I thought was a temporary sense of happiness. In reality, though, it just fueled the misery growing inside of me. I was emotionally and spiritually bankrupt without any clear vision where my life would take me. I was in a constant war with myself in my head. The feeling was unbearable at times. It took a close call with death due to alcohol poisoning and cocaine, along with hitting rock bottom emotionally and spiritually, for me to surrender.

When I made the decision to surrender and seek help, my life completely changed, success took on a whole new meaning, and I finally found joy and happiness. Money also soon followed, but it was no longer what I perceived to be my "why." Instead I discovered that my true calling was empowering and helping others find their way. It was about assisting others through change and adding value wherever possible. This became my "why"—a "why" that brought joy and happiness.

I have coached many clients who have dreams of starting a business. While this is a worthy goal, starting a business has to be congruent with a person's core values and true purpose. The by-products of success, such as money and material things, are great, but they will never sustain a business if they are the primary reason. Your reason for success has to be bigger than materialistic objects. Your vision for business has to focus on your core values and how it will impact others for good. During economic ups and downs in business, which are inevitable, you will always stay the course based on your vision of true purpose in alignment to the value you bring to others with your goods and services. It is this premise that will drive you each day to succeed and deliver more value to others. Your work will not seem like a drag—every day of the week will be fun and have meaning, even on weekends. Defining your core values and revising your plan or vision as required will enable you to master the craft of delivering value. The key is to not focus on setting goals, but from focusing on your "why" so your energy generates from joy and happiness toward a purposeful life. When you truly understand your "why," motivation is often effortless because it is fueled by joy and happiness. Your purpose is what will set you apart from the competition and allow you to add continuous value to customers and prospects. True success cannot truly exist without having fulfillment tied to your purpose. Remember, doing something for money will only get you so far before it fades to black.

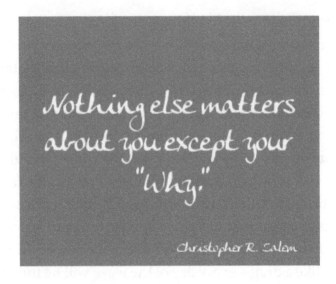

Nothing else matters about you except your "Why."

Christopher R. Salem

How do you find your "why"? How do you know when you've found it? The following steps will assist you to answer these questions.

1) Be happy—ask yourself: "What makes me happy?"
   This is a question that requires some quiet time to reflect and write down what comes to mind as depicted earlier in this chapter. What brings you joy and happiness? Be real with yourself and come from your inner critic, not someone else's perception of you. This is not about what your parents, coaches, or other adults thought when you were growing up. This is about you and only

you. The key here is not to just write down what makes you happy, but to go even deeper with it. Drill deeper with other questions that either support what makes your happy or does not. There is no set amount of sub-questions—only as many as required to justify your true feeling. Think of it as proving your hypothesis by supporting it with examples and facts. You have found your purpose when it brings a smile to your face and you feel clear and light inside. If you have trouble finding it, just stick with it; this is not a race. Finding your purpose may require trial and error to find it.

2) Know your strengths—ask yourself: "What are my strengths?"

Focus on your strengths. Write them down and spend time figuring out how this plays into your "why." You should know your weaknesses as well, but spend your time fully focusing on your strengths. Too many people spend time overanalyzing their weaknesses and looking for ways to improve them.

Forgot about this and spend your time thinking about enhancing your strengths. Putting your strengths to work as it correlates with your purpose will bring tremendous value to others and set you apart from others in your business. Spending time on your weaknesses will not make this happen. If you are unsure about your strengths, one great resource is the Gallup Strengths Finder (www.gallupstrengthscenter.com).

3) Be in the flow—ask yourself: "Am I truly in the flow?"

You have heard the term "being in the zone." This is flow. It is being completely absorbed in the moment. It's doing something and being fully immersed, laser-focused, all in, and truly enjoying the process. When you are in the flow, it allows positive emotions such as joy and happiness to radiate outward from within, attracting positive energy that brings your purpose to full light. Allow yourself to be in the moment without internal judgment from the negative side of your Inner Critic. When you are doing something bigger than you that brings pure joy from your core, that's when you know you have found your calling or life mission.

Set Goals to Live Life on Your Terms

"A goal is a dream with a deadline."

Napoleon Hill

When you know your "why" and truly embrace your purpose, you can live life on your own terms while providing value to others. Specific, attainable goals are required, because without specific goals, your plan is directionless. Some people have gone through the hard steps discussed previously in this book, but then did not write down attainable, executable goals in order to truly fulfill their "why." They may know their purpose but have not been specific enough about how to fulfill it. The process has to be specific and written down on paper. Ask yourself, would you set out to explore a new career or hobby without knowing the specifics required for it? The answer is probably no.

Goal-setting is a powerful process that requires each step to be specific for fulfilling your purpose. It requires wisdom, not just vision, to see the big picture from a broader perspective so you can turn your goals into reality. The process of setting attainable goals helps you to be organized, structured, and accountable toward your chosen path. When you know precisely where you want to go in life, specific goals allow you to keep focused on the efforts needed to get you there. Goals help build self-confidence and awareness, thus lowering stress and anxiety when you encounter obstacles that test your commitment. Being specific also means that distractions and engaging in procrastination are easy to identify.

How Do You Set Personal Attainable Goals?
This is a process that starts with looking at the big picture first and then drilling down to smaller attainable goals within a designated, specific time frame. Each step holds you accountable toward reaching the big picture in life.

- Define your long-term life goal for fulfilling your purpose. Look at the larger goals that will help you to accomplish your purpose. Give it a deadline, such as five years.

- Break down your long-term goal into smaller, more attainable goals over the specified time period. For example, if the larger goal is five years, then smaller goals will be broken down into years and months.

- Once your plan is clearly defined with every details specific to the big picture captured, then begin to work each of these smaller goals in sequence, keeping yourself accountable.

Remember that your vision is to see the end result—the big picture—but wisdom is required to set small, attainable goals with deadlines in order to get you there. You must be accountable at all times.

GOALS START IN THE CORE OF YOUR ESSENCE, THEN ARE DEFINED IN WORDS SPECIFIC TO EACH DETAIL, AND FINALLY FULFILLED WITH TIMELY EXECUTABLE ACTION.

Christopher R. Salem

Set Long-Term Life Goals
Ask yourself what you want to achieve in your life from this moment forward. Be specific about the littlest detail and set a realistic time frame. Setting long-term life goals will provide you with a vision of what is required

to fulfill your purpose. It will influence your decision-making and keep you focused on reaching your goals while you enjoy every step of the journey.

To begin, look at the eight pillars of wellness to map how to create a life that fulfills your purpose. Set specific goals in each category that are important to you. The key is to find excellence with balance, not perfection. Be specific again by writing out answers to the questions below, and then make a commitment to be accountable to each one.

- **Occupational** – What do I want to do? What gives me purpose? What are my creative attributes, and how can I use them to add value to others? Does my career truly add value to others? What do I ultimately want to achieve?

- **Financial** – What does wealth mean to me? How much do I want to earn, by what stage? Am I open to new ideas, such as learning to live debt-free, live below my means, investing, and residual income ideas? What do I want to do with my money?

- **Intellectual** – What knowledge is required to fulfill my purpose? What resources or education are required to enhance my skills and strengths to achieve my long-term life goals?

- **Social** – What do I like about myself? How do I want to enjoy my life? What is the value I offer to others—family, friends, customers, and coworkers? What skills do I require to connect better with people, form better relationships, and be a better spouse and parent?

- **Emotional** – Do my new healthier habits and behaviors align with my purpose? Do I have the right mindset and attitude to see the solution behind problems or challenges? Do I detach myself from the outcome of any situation and come from a place of peace?

- **Physical** – What can I change to feed my body with the right balance of nutrition? Am I making better choices about taking care of my body and mind through a proper balance of supernutrition and exercise? What steps are necessary to live a long, healthy life, free of sickness?

- **Spiritual** – Does my life have meaning and purpose aligned with the Universe, or with my faith? Are my actions and commitment to my faith of choice consistent with my values and beliefs?

- **Environmental** – Do I want to make the world a healthier and better place? If so, how?

Spend time addressing these questions from your heart. Take your time and be honest with yourself. These are *your* goals to achieve, not those of your family, friends, or coworkers. Select one or more goals from each category as it applies to your true purpose with your long-term life goal. Next, revise where needed so you can begin to focus on one or two from each category.

Set Smaller, More Attainable Goals

Your long-term life goals will be achieved by carefully planned and executed smaller, attainable goals. Set a five-year plan for smaller, attainable goals that are specific to each detail necessary to bring your big picture to fruition. Break out these smaller goals into a one-year plan, a six-month plan, and a one-month plan; these time periods will hold you accountable and motivate you toward your long-term life goals. Each of these should be based on the previous plan. A daily "to-do" list on paper (preferred), smartphone, or tablet will keep you on track each day. Paper is preferred because when you write something by hand, it clicks in your brain, and you're more likely to follow through with the daily action required. It is highly encouraged during the early stages of working on smaller, attainable goals to include a goal of personal development. This would include books, mastermind groups, and listening to webinars that enhance one's knowledge and skills. This will greatly improve not only the quality of your goal-setting but also carrying them out; it will prevent distractions and procrastination from derailing you. Make sure you review the plan during every phase to make sure it is aligned to your long-term life goals and fulfills your true purpose.

This is a live process, so stay the course until you reach the big picture. You can modify the plan if required as you accomplish each smaller set of goals. Plan to have daily reviews to reflect on your experience with this process and make any adjustments. A great way to make your goals more impactful is by using SMART goals.

SMART stands for:

- **S** – Specific

- **M** – Measurable

- **A** – Attainable

- **R** – Relevant

- **T** – Timely

Let's look at an example of how SMART goals work. Instead of having "to travel around the world" as a goal, it's more impactful to use a SMART goal: "To complete my travel around the world by December 31, 2017." You can see this goal is specific, measurable, attainable, relevant, and has a time frame for being accomplished. This goal is more likely to be attained because there is more preparation behind it coupled with action. Here are some other guidelines to make your smaller, attainable goals more effective:

- **Write your goals down on paper.** This solidifies them from your true inner purpose and gives you the energy to execute them. Writing is powerful, so do not interject technology into this step.

- **Be specific.** State your goal, down to every detail and with a time frame for it to be completed. Specific written details provide energy and executable action.

- **Use a positive statement with each goal.** Words are powerful and dictate the level of energy, whether positive or negative, when carrying them out. Be conscious of this fact. For example, "I will become the CEO on January 1, 2018" is positive, whereas "I will not make the mistakes in the past that can hinder my progress toward CEO status" is a negative statement.

- **Set smaller, attainable goals.** These goals should be realistic or ones that with effort can be achieved. Follow your true purpose means you can raise the bar, but make sure any goals are realistically achievable. It is important to keep your goals small and incremental, thus creating more opportunities for reward.

- **Set priorities.** Each of your smaller, attainable goals should be given a priority rank. This helps to keep you focused, organized, and not feeling overwhelmed by having too many goals.

- **Practice detachment and acceptance.** Learn to detach yourself from the outcome and set performance goals instead. Setting performance goals provides you with more control versus being attached to the outcome. It allows you to see the solution behind the problem so you can forge ahead with your goals.

Examples of Small, Attainable Goals
Jennifer has a made a choice to become an entrepreneur who runs her own insurance agency.

Her long-term life goals are:

- **Occupational** – "To be the CEO/president of my own insurance agency in three years."

- **Financial** – "To become a millionaire in five years by using residual income streams from insurance business and investments."

- **Physical** – "To be at my high-school weight and have more energy in two years through a consistent routine of supernutrition along with a resistance/cardio program."

Next, Jennifer then breaks down each goal into smaller, more manageable, attainable goals:

- **Five-year goal:** "Become a millionaire."

- **Three-year goal:** "Become CEO/president of my insurance agency."

- **Two-year goals:**

  - "Be at my high school weight and have more consistent energy."

- "Work for an insurance agency to learn the business of managing an agency and the art of leveraging through agents."

- "Invest 30 percent of my income toward investments and master the skill of residual income models."

- **One-year goals:**

  - "Run first mini-marathon."

  - "Become the number-one producer in the insurance agency as a CEO protégé."

  - "Save 25 percent of my income from work and residual income streams."

- **Six-month goals:**

  - "Release fifty pounds gradually and stay the course toward my physical goal."

  - "Obtain certifications and other knowledge required to position me toward CEO/president status."

- "Have one or two residual income models working efficiently to produce ongoing income."

- **One-month goals:**

  - "Start at a gym or fitness center that I feel comfortable with to implement resistance-cardio component to my supernutrition program."

  - "Spend extra time each day in the office to learn the ropes from another CEO/president of insurance agency."

  - "Set up my financial plan toward millionaire status and read valuable information to get me there for up to twenty hours each month."

- **One-week goals:**

  - "Obtain information on what foods provide optimal supernutrition."

  - "Connect and interview with insurance agencies to choose one that best supports my long-term goal."

- "Find sources and begin to compile contacts that can help educate me on learning systems that create millionaires."

As you can see from this example, breaking long-term life goals down into smaller, more manageable or attainable goals provides a clear structure and makes it easier to see how the goal will get accomplished. Without a clearly defined plan, it is impossible to master your goals fully! It is important to keep reviewing and making modifications to your long term life goals whenever required. This is a process, so enjoy the journey. There is no race here, so just keep yourself accountable by moving forward and accomplishing each small, attainable goal. Celebrate when you reach each smaller goal; this keeps your momentum going. Remember, you are here to play big, not small, in life. Your Inner Critic will speak to you in both large and small ways. Your job is to listen to the right advice it gives you about playing big. When the root cause is removed and action is taken toward the necessary steps to embrace change, step outside of your comfort zone, and work toward your larger life goals, self-confidence and awareness take over and help you make the right choice.

Questions to Ask Your Inner Critic

What is your specific long-term life goal?

What are your smaller, attainable goals (broken out as follows)? Be specific.

Five Years?

Three Years?

Two Years?

One Year?

Six Months?

One Month?

One Week?

STEP 6

Invest in Yourself

"Investing in yourself is the best investment you will ever make. It will not only improve your life; it will improve the lives of all those around you."

Robin S. Sharma

You have probably heard before that there is no greater investment than in yourself. However, many people fail to make themselves a priority, especially when it comes to their overall wellness and personal development. It is this step that sustains everything you've done to master your inner critic throughout the rest of your life. When there is no balance with one's wellness and personal development, it is difficult to maintain continued strides towards mastery of your Inner Critic. This is where the negative side of your Inner Critic can creep up and take control, causing a relapse or decline in mastery.

My father devoted all his energy and intelligence to building a successful business that helped diabetics test their glucose through a popular testing kit. He was very smart and used every waking moment to fulfill this venture. However, his purpose was off— his life was unbalanced and it cost him dearly. While physically he was in good shape, he lacked the ability to address his emotional and spiritual wellness. This lack of balance coupled with living in the effect and not resolving the root cause led to great stress in his life. My father never took care of himself fully, and while he had significant accomplishments with patents and business success, these were not as important as the big picture. His accomplishments coupled with taking good care of himself would have been a positive example to his family and associates. Empowerment is truly the greatest gift, and the value offered is endless.

This was the case for me in my early adult years as well. I was physically in good shape, but I failed to address my emotional and spiritual wellness. This was before I addressed and resolved the root cause that plagued me. My priorities were way off; I was focused on working out, which was good, but I was striving to make money without addressing other important wellness areas in my life. This unbalance combined with a large intake of calories to build muscle and stress from heavy weight-lifting led to a strange growth on my back. This growth was just underneath the skin, growing aggressively, and beginning to attach to my spinal column. It was removed several times without success by doctors from various hospitals, including specialty centers. It would grow back in a matter of a few weeks.

This experience finally became a textbook case treated at Memorial Sloan Kettering Cancer Center. Over a six-month period, the doctors there treated this tumor as though it were a form of an aggressive cancer, including radical surgery to remove muscles that were impacting certain nerves, resulting in a lack of feeling in certain areas of my back. While doctors and researchers could not pinpoint what caused the tumor, they classified it as a desmoids tumor. In hindsight, it is my belief that this tumor was the result of imbalances in my emotional and spiritual life combined with too many calories being ingested daily and the heaving lifting that severely stressed my body.

My anecdote is the reality of many: The majority of us seldom put ourselves first. We invest in the latest appliances and gadgets to organize/complicate our lives, hopeful business ventures, and other people's dreams. We dress according to trends and style our hair from what we see in magazines. But are we doing what we love, or do we love conforming to the whims of the world? Are we truly free, or is our freedom entirely dependent on the impressions of others?

Honestly answer these three questions:

When was the last time I did something I love or felt passionate about?

What have I done currently to better myself in terms of wellness and personal development?

What sources do I consider valuable to listen to for advice?

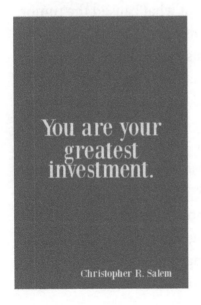

You are your greatest investment.

Christopher R. Salem

Your honest answers to these questions will provide you with a better understanding of how your energy is used. It may be serving you—or perhaps not. If it's not serving you, having the awareness to change this is important. After addressing these questions, if you feel compelled that self-care is what you desire to raise the bar with your overall wellness and personal development, then make it a priority to invest in yourself using the following suggestions.

1. Make Your Self-Worth a Priority. Never assume that being in a good place or having high self-esteem will always happen without practice. You should always work to improve yourself by focusing on your strengths so your inner dialogue speaks more positive things than negative. Again, this should never be taken this for granted. Resolving your "root cause" will help to heal old wounds and release perceived fears and insecurities.

Self-worth is attractive to others; it empowers them. It is not selfish, but rather delivers value to others continuously. For example, a mother who works hard to improve her quality of health by eating clean whole foods and participating in a consistent workout routine to release significant weight offers more value to her family, especially to her kids. She is an example to her family, and by taking care of herself, she can spend quality time with them. Putting herself last and always doing everything for her family does not serve them long-term. Empowering them through her example benefits their growth in so many ways—from learning to take care of themselves, adopting healthier habits, and spending quality time with one another.

2. Be Your Best Friend—Be True to Who You Are. It is important to accept who you are with all your strengths and weaknesses. You are may not always connect with everyone, but you will connect with those that see the value you bring to them. Always strive to be of value to yourself and others. You are both perfect and flawed—a unique combination that can never be replicated—and this fact should be embraced. When you truly love yourself in an unselfish way, you empower others to focus on improving their own well-being. It becomes contagious in a good way, leading to great changes and positive development in people.

3. Always Trust Your Intuition. Your intuition is a specialized intelligence unit that knows you better than anyone else. It knows more than you perceive. Strive to trust your inner voice without hesitation. Over-thinking something only creates confusion. Being self-aware along with being quiet and calm allows you to tap into this specialized intelligence unit in order to receive the right answer. It is important not to second-guess your decision; go with the flow with what your intuition tells you. This works well for those that have fully addressed and resolved the "root cause" in their lives. Your intuition is your best friend and is always looking out to protect you and do what is right for your well-being.

4. Go for Your True Requirements Versus What Your Wants. Everyone has unique requirements. Notice that I use the word *requirements* instead of *needs*. The word *need* has no action behind it, but *requirement* does have action. Look at what you require that plays to your strengths and makes your life meaningful to yourself and others. You may find that when you address and fulfill your requirements that what you perceived you wanted will fade into the sunset. There is freedom and a sense of lightness in our well-being when we focus on our true requirements versus our wants.

5. Raise the Bar toward Your Better Self. Life will always present plateaus and obstacles. These are tests to your commitment to yourself as you strive for excellence. Never settle for mediocrity—growth and good things can never materialize without raising the bar with yourself. Visualize what you want to become and bring your thoughts, spoken words, and actions together to work congruently toward manifesting them into reality. Only you can limit you, and it all starts with your thoughts. When you fully address the "root cause" and release it, this process becomes easier as you become your own best friend. Self-confidence increases and positive thinking prevails over the negative with your Inner Critic.

6. Do What You Love. Your true self knows what it loves—listen to it. Commit to fulfilling what it says; your joy not only helps you but empowers others. It is a gift that keeps on giving and is contagious. Do not put off doing what you love until tomorrow—begin to implement it today! Watch how consistent joy and happiness fill up the space that once were consumed with shame, guilt, and anger. Seeing this in you also sets the example for others to follow suit.

7. Take Care of Your Vessel. It is imperative that you take care of yourself by eating clean, wholesome foods with a low glycemic index and free of GMO and pesticides. Always look for organic foods from local farms if possible and implement supernutrition from trusted sources that use whole foods and herbs (nothing synthetic) to keep the body operating at peak efficiency. Keep in mind that supernutrition in the form of supplements is not considered high quality, especially when bought through retail market or stores. It is best to obtain supplements directly from the manufacturer, as this often signals better quality and value. There are trusted sources out there to assist you with options that best serve you. Find and seek them out.

Balance nutrition with a resistance/cardio training program where 60 to 65 percent is resistance training and 35 to 40 percent is cardio. Please note that resistance training is better overall than cardio, but a balanced combination works well to enhance the quality nutrition you put into body. This goes for women as well, who often just do cardio and skip resistance training. *Only you can take care of you.* Many people place this responsibility with their doctor or healthcare practitioner. These professionals are there to help you, but they will never be able to look out for your best interests entirely. Self-care *always* starts and ends with you. Adopt these healthy habits and watch yourself grow stronger each day.

8. Be the Example for Others. There is no greater gift than empowerment. Being an example to others means doing things that serve you in a positive way and radiate positive energy to others that observe what you do. When you set an example, you show those around you that you've invested in yourself time and time again to reach a level of excellence. Remember, putting yourself first is not selfish—it's doing something positive that propels you toward success. It empowers others to potentially do the same, which is far better than doing it for them. Success is a process. Jim Rohn always said, "It is what you become in the process that is true success." Trust the process—what you become is the greatest feeling of all.

9. Expand Your Wealth. While building wealth monetarily is important, there is no greater wealth than having knowledge, wisdom, and compassion. When you are armed with this true wealth, there is nothing that will stop you from overcoming the inevitable challenges on the way to becoming successful. Knowing this allows you to grow, and applying it brings wealth. It is how you feel inside that comes from applying the knowledge, wisdom, and compassion to create wealth.

STEP 7

Be Accountable

"Accountability breeds response-ability."

Stephen R. Covey

Nothing in life can be carried out to the fullest without accountability! It is the one ingredient to this process that glues all these steps together in order to make a new you come to fruition. Accountability means living in integrity, with all your thoughts, words, and actions are consistent with one another and in alignment. Commitment is one thing, but accountability is vital to sustaining long-term success and mastering your Inner Critic. When one is accountable, he or she accepts responsibility for his or her actions and the results of his or her choices in life. Your actions always have consequences, whether good or bad. It is your choice to make sure your thoughts, words, and actions are working synergistically together in a positive way to manifest the results you desire to create with yourself. The key is taking ownership for your part in the process, being accountable for what you can control, and accepting what you cannot.

Accountability starts off in the right direction when you commit to the process from the beginning by acknowledging where you are now and being aware of the reality of your situation. When you acknowledge the truth about where you are now and how you truly feel, you then have the ability to execute the steps outlined in this book. It is very important one accept ownership by acknowledging where you are at the moment. Without ownership, accountability cannot sustain itself! The process of acknowledging and accepting responsibility for yourself allows you to seek solutions found in the steps we've discussed and apply the right ones for true change and sustainable success. This also empowers and invigorates you to go for it and see it through despite any obstacles or setbacks that happen along the way.

The process of accountability also prevents you from falling prey to the victim role. It prevents you from being unaware of how you feel or where you are right now. You are more likely not to complain during the process since acceptance helps to alleviate this negative action. Again, it cannot be stated enough that the collaboration of acknowledgment and acceptance in tandem is what will keep you focused on your results without allowing excuses to enter the process. This is not bulletproof, but it helps create awareness about making the positive choices that lead to positive actions. Finally, accountability keeps you focused on the process of change and following through all the steps required. It keeps you in positive action as you watch this process play out.

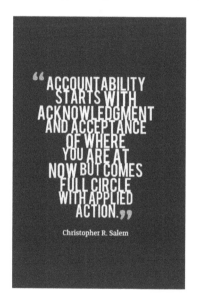

It was accountability that kept me on track when I went through the process of mastering my Inner Critic several years ago. It was not just starting with acknowledgment and acceptance of my situation; it was also having an accountability partner from the beginning. This person was my sponsor, a term 12-Step groups use for someone to keep individuals accountable to change. However, it also included the 12-Step group itself; this was my mastermind group where I came to terms with my demons and became accountable to my sponsor and others that were going or had gone through this process. My sponsor was a humble man who had experienced situations with his father that were similar to mine. This included dealing with anger issues and living from the false self, which led to a life of misery.

We all are different in terms of how we handle and execute change in our lives. Some have more discipline than others. However, despite these differences, it is imperative that we all have accountability partners. Someone with a similar background or past experiences allows you to relate to each other easily, but it's not required in order to be successful with this process. A person who is unbiased and neutral can be just as effective—or in some cases better, depending upon one's experiences and background. It is important to go with your gut and align with someone with whom you feel comfortable and can trust to empower and assist you toward being accountable. A coach or mentor also works well, especially if they are unbiased and neutral (even if they had similar experiences or background similar to yours in the past).

Being held accountable to someone was terrifying for me back then because I had never allowed myself to trust anyone in that position after my father failed to be that person for me. I perceived myself to be accountable for my actions before this process began, but my false self continued to lie to me, and in reality I could not even trust myself. How could I trust others to hold me accountable when I did not trust myself? This was the reality, but my false self created the illusion that I was in control and accountable for my actions. It took more than merely acknowledging of my current state and owning it when I was going through this process. The guidance of an accountability partner through empowerment played a huge part in carrying out this process. I did the work, but the empowerment factor through my sponsor and mastermind group were instrumental to bring it full circle.

The accountability factor is the glue that holds everything together. A combination of both a neutral accountability partner and mastermind (support) group is highly encouraged. The accountability partner could be a friend that is neutral to your situation, an unbiased third-party person that you do not know well but feel comfortable about him or her being your coach or trusted adviser. The mastermind or support group solidifies this process, providing added support to address your issues and find your solutions. Both working in tandem will yield far greater results with this element of the process. This accountability team will:

- Empower you to acknowledge, accept, and then release the root cause

- Assist you to come up with smaller, attainable goals to achieve positive change in order to realize your core objective or long-term life goal

- Hold you accountable to the list of actions required to fulfill your objective and set a time limit for each task

- Remind you when action steps are not completed and achieved by deadline dates

- Keep you on course toward achieving your long-term goal

Can you do this? You have the strength to do more than you know when you really want or desire to change. It starts with acknowledgement and acceptance, which means taking ownership for being a slave to your root cause. You do not have to be a slave to your root cause any more—taking ownership leads to having more control over your actions as you resolve and release it. You have accepted personal responsibility by holding yourself—and no one else—accountable. Your support team gives you an empowered approach to this process of making positive changes.

Accountability is a friend of your Inner Critic; it always seeks solutions for bettering yourself. It does not allow for complaining—you have the power to take control over the actions you can control and let go of the rest. There is no one to blame now except yourself if for any reason you deviate off course. The good news is you can always hop back on track and move forward. Accountability expands your ability to problem solve or resolve the root cause and move forward in consistent fashion toward your desired outcome. When coupled with responsibility, you can take full ownership of your life. It is not always peaches and cream, but more often than not it leads to positive change and healthier relationships.

In addition, your business or career will vastly improve with accountability in place. It builds trust from the foundation and healthier interactions with team members and customers. Follow-through with tasks and projects become more efficient because accountability keeps you on course to fulfill your commitments. It also plays a vital role in reducing fear because trust increases teams to pull together toward achieving their goals. It also will increase your creativity and innovation toward new ideas that add value to others. Productivity increases as a result of more efficient processes, thus saving on costs and creating more time for innovation. Work becomes fun again as you get along with others to create great things together.

Accountability is not about perfection. It may not always deliver what you want, but it will always deliver what you require. It allows you to operate with integrity in terms of your choices and actions working synergistically together. Accountability empowers you to be in control of your actions in your personal and business life. You can create your own opportunities rather than passively allowing life to happen around you. Accountability is contagious and empowers others to reach for optimal success. Be the example and lead others by empowering them to go through this process of being accountable! A truly authentic leader empowers others.

Questions to Ask Your Inner Critic

Who are people you know that are completely unbiased and would be open to being your accountability partner?

What mastermind or support groups align with the values and solutions you seek as part of the accountability process?

Are you 100 percent committed to acknowledge and accept ownership of being accountable and following through with this process?

Are You Ready?

You are the common denominator when you decide to truly resolve and let go of the root cause. A life better than where you are now cannot be accomplished or be sustainable without resolving the root cause that created the effects that hold you back. Pushing that root cause further down into your core and working around it with success and other personal development principles will come up short unless you commit to going through this process. The main question to ask yourself upon reading these steps is: "Am I truly ready"?

If you are truly ready, it is time to experience the journey of finding your true self. Once you have identified the root cause of your particular addiction—remember, everybody has one—you can focus on developing a better quality of life. Using self-empowerment, you can go from your unhealthy state of mind to a healthier, happier place where you will reduce the need to self-soothe through unhealthy habits and behaviors that do not serve you. So the question is, are you ready? Let's look at model below to help you determine where you are in this process of addressing your root cause.

Several years ago, two researchers in the area of addiction, Carlo C. DiClemente and J. O. Prochaska, put into play a six-stage model of change to help professionals in this area better understand their clients with addiction problems.[1] In addition, it gave them insight into how to motivate change within their clients toward adopting healthier, more sustainable habits. Their model is based not on abstract theories, but on their personal observations of how people went about modifying problem behaviors such as overeating, smoking, and problem drinking.

The six stages of the model are:

- Pre-contemplation

- Contemplation

- Determination

- Action

- Maintenance

- Termination

1 Sources: *Changing for Good,* J. Prochaska, Norcross, and C. Di Clemente (New York: William Morrow, 1994); *The Transtheoretical Approach: Crossing the Traditional Boundaries of Therapy,* J. Prochaska and C. Di Clemente (Malabar, Fla.: Krieger Publishing Company, 1984).

This six-stage model is what I used in conjunction with an accountability sponsor along with a support group when I decided to address my addiction and then resolve my root cause. Addiction was the effect and result of my root cause (the lack of connection with my father). Please note: you do not have to be an addict to benefit from this model. We all have certain habits and behaviors that are not healthy or do not serve us long-term. The model will help you understand options that are best for you as you prepare for change. While this model is designed first to address the addiction itself, it also prepares you to fully commit toward resolving your root cause. I will explain how this six-stage model works as it relates to the root cause, not just addiction. Also note that some people may not be in the pre-contemplation stage as they have already acknowledged there is a problem. Therefore, they may fall under the contemplation or determination stage as part of this model.

Pre-contemplation

People in this stage of change are not even thinking about changing their addictive behavior. They may not personally see their addiction as a problem and are often not receptive to others that point out their issues.

There are four key reasons to be in pre-contemplation stage. Dr. DiClemente classifies them as "the Four Rs" —reluctance, rebellion, resignation, and rationalization.

- Reluctant pre-contemplators do not want to consider change due to lack of knowledge or ignorance of their root cause. They are not fully conscious or aware of the impact of their problem.

- Rebellious pre-contemplators do not like to be told what to do and are not yet open to suggestions for change.

- Resigned pre-contemplators are overly consumed in their root cause or problem and feel they have no hope or possibility of change.

- Rationalizing pre-contemplators are always right and are not willing to admit that their habits and behavior are a problem.

Contemplation
People in this stage of change understand on some level that their problem has a negative effect on their life and others. They have not fully acknowledged their problem, but the way they feel inside provides some possibility for change. However, people here are always

on the fence because they have not fully acknowledged the problem in their life; they have not yet bottomed out in order to make a commitment to change. They are only interested in seeking information about the problem.

It should be noted that people in this stage may work with a professional or themselves to conduct a risk-reward analysis. They consider the pros and cons of their behavior as a result of their problem as well as the pros and cons of change. They acknowledge on some level what they have done to overcome their problem and what has failed to fix it.

This was the stage I was in when I entered this process. I had already stopped the habits of binge drinking, using recreational drugs, promiscuous sex, and working out too much a year earlier, but had not yet acknowledged the behaviors that were the effects of my root cause. During this stage I was aware on some level that my behaviors were not serving me long term. I also realized that my behavior was affecting others around me. The good news was that I hit rock bottom emotionally and spiritually during the period between stopping the bad habits and acknowledging the problems with my behavior. The only way out was up, and this meant making a decision to change. Hitting rock bottom shortly thereafter pushed me over the fence to take action and move to the next stage, determination.

Determination

This is the stage where a commitment is made to change. This is where people decide to stop bad habits and begin to release bad behaviors for good. A risk-reward analysis has been done in favor of change. There may still be some ambivalence as in the Contemplation stage, but it no longer holds the power to prevent change. People in this stage are ready and committed to action.

This stage requires preparation along with determination. A realistic plan is necessary here since commitment to change without appropriate skills and activities creates the likelihood for failure. It is during this stage—whether someone is addressing an addiction or one's root cause—that one devises a realistic assessment for solving the problem. Individuals often will work with a professional or accountability partner or group to come up with solutions necessary to address obstacles and pitfalls that will present itself during the process.

Action

People in this stage are committed to implementing their plan and putting it into action. This stage usually involves transparency—to not only their accountability partners but also to a group of people—about the common denominator of causes that led to their root cause. Making a public commitment holds people accountable to their commitment. This helps people in terms of external support with accountability and provides a sense of comfort while they are stepping out of their comfort zones. There will be always people, sometimes even family, that may hope you "fall off the wagon" because they are also not in a good place. For those who address their addiction or the deeper root cause behind it, one of the many pleasures is disproving the negative predictions of others.

Success comes from persistence, action, and accountability in executing a plan. For those committed to change, the obstacles that will come from their addiction and root cause can be minimized as hope and self-confidence fill the empty hole inside their core. People are able to replace unhealthy habits and behaviors with wholesome ones. Better yet, these new habits become sustainable over time by consistently following their plan.

Maintenance
The action stage takes anywhere from three to six months to complete. When it comes to change, it requires time to establish new, sustainable habits and

behaviors. The real test of change is long-term sustained change over many years. If people become complacent or begin resting on their laurels, they can relapse. This is the case with an addict as well as those who have struggled in life as a result of their root cause. This stage of successful change is called "maintenance." In this stage, a new life free of one's root cause is established. A maintenance plan of personal development strengthens and maintains one's well-being while minimizing the likelihood that old habits and behaviors will return. New habits and behaviors practiced daily through the maintenance stage assist in keeping old patterns at bay, and they become less intense and frequent. People in this stage are equipped now with better life skills which enable them to avoid returning to old patterns that did not serve them. The key is to stay in the moment each day, which requires practice. If someone relapses, this is not always a bad thing. Failure is when someone quits, and sometimes relapses may be necessary to see where one once was and where he or she is now. It will be easier to see how one feels in both places during the course of one's life. It is always better, once experienced, to live in the solution to one's root cause and not in its effects.

Termination
This is the stage where anyone who has struggled with addiction or other issues desires to be. It is here that people find sustainable comfort in their own skin, where the root cause no longer presents a temptation and self-confidence through consistent personal development keeps one in check.

Susan's Journey
A woman I coached a while ago was in the Contemplation stage. We will call her Susan. She was confused about how her life had been up to this point but had not yet fully acknowledged the problem. She knew something was off and felt life could be better. This moved her to the Determination stage, and she made a commitment to identify and release the root cause and then adopt a plan that would create a better life for her and her family.

As an only child, her parents encouraged her to be active in and out of school. She was involved in Girl Scouts and gymnastics. While she did her best, she did not do as well as her parents had hoped. When she was fourteen, her parents divorced. They had been arguing since she was seven, and despite the fact that they tried to hide it, there was no denying the impact it had on her. She was sad during this time and devastated after the divorce.

Her personal identity was in crisis, and she thought her parent's divorce was her fault because she wasn't living up to her parents' expectations.

The results of her parents' divorce led to much confusion throughout Susan's adult life. She basically drifted through college without any clear direction. She had two children as a single parent and worked in retail to support her family. Men would come and go in her life; she was never able to trust any of them enough to have a serious relationship. Her mom did help her but still would keep her at arm's length by not letting her get too close.

It was determined during our coaching sessions that the activities she participated in after school as a result of her parent's wishes actually never interested her. She felt these activities distracted her from reading and studying, which at the time she really loved. She tried to keep the balance of doing well in school and participate in these activities only to fall short of her parents' expectations. She cited feeling shame for letting her parents down. Now that she was an adult, she understood that the dissolution of her parents' marriage was not her fault, but her subconscious mind believed otherwise and prevented her from building the life she deserved.

The emotion of shame led Susan to experience low self-esteem and low self-confidence, which was the effect. Her parents' high expectation that she perform well was the cause. Both parents were the root cause of her feelings of shame and guilt over her parents' divorce. Living in the effect prevented her from getting close to a man; she feared subconsciously that she would let him down and cause him leave the relationship.

Susan was able to acknowledge and accept her root cause and commit to the process of releasing it from her subconscious mind. She was now at the Determination stage and truly wanted to release it, even though the process was not easy. She recognized that to go on living this way would have a negative impact on her children. She learned to forgive her parents and made the commitment to herself to excel in both her career and her personal life. This meant embracing change and stepping into her fear in order to release her old thinking subconsciously and replace with thoughts, habits, and behaviors that come from joy, happiness, and confidence. She would no longer live in the effect of shame with self-doubt and a lack of confidence.

We put together a long-term life goal—to obtain her law degree and have a successful practice. Another part of this long term life goal was to provide to provide more to her children, do something she really had passion for, and help families requiring legal advice. She was able to do this over a three-year period by focusing on each time frame with smaller, attainable goals while raising her children and working to make ends meet. Susan clearly made an investment in herself to improve her life and the lives of everyone around her. She stayed accountable to herself and joined a support group to keep her focused. The strength and resolve she acquired during this time opened doors full of incredible opportunities. She graduated near the top of her class in law school and was hired by a local firm with a specialty in family matters.

She also knew having a stable relationship with a man was good for her and her children. She recognized during this process that she did not trust *herself*, and this is why she avoided relationships. She was able to develop self-trust during the coaching process along with a belief that she deserved to receive love and happiness as well as give it. She waited patiently and met her true soulmate just before graduation from law school.

Susan overcame her fears from her past and stepped beyond her self-doubts. After dating for a year, she became engaged. Even with all the challenges that life threw her way, she was living her dream! She now enjoys a successful career, a loving, supportive husband, and healthy, happy children.

Your Turn

So where do you fall on this six-stage model? Remember, you do not have to be an addict to use this model. Everyone has vices or engages in something that does not serve them in a healthy way. Living in the effect of one's root cause is the reason people adapt to bad habits and behaviors in order to mask the problem or pain. Be honest with yourself and determine which stage aligns with where you are today. Use this as a guide with an accountability partner and/or group along with the suggestions presented in this book.

Ten Steps to Eliminate, Reduce, or Minimize Self-Doubt

1. Address and confront the root cause(s) that led to the effects that create self-doubt, and truly let them go through forgiveness.

2. Make the conscious choice to change and embrace success by looking at it as a journey and growth process, not a destination.

3. Incorporate a daily schedule of meditation, personal development, clean eating, and exercise to create balance and overall well-being. Important

life decisions are best made when grounded and coming from a sense of peace, joy, happiness, and feeling of confidence.

4. Always be grateful for where you are now and where you are going.

5. Be in the present moment and know that fear manifests itself when you dwell too much on the past and project too much into the future.

6. Come out of your comfort zone early and be willing to be consistent, but never strive for perfection when it comes to adopting new habits that best serve you on your journey toward success. Never become complacent; the greatest growth comes from outside your comfort zone.

7. Write down short-term and long-term goals and set attainable goals over time. Reward yourself in a positive way for each goal met along the way.

8. Recognize your fear and never label it as a feeling of nervousness or anxiety.

9. Always remember that you only fail if you do not start or do not follow through. If something does

not work during this journey, see it as a learning experience and part of the process toward achieving something better. The Universe will test you, and when you make the choice to really go for it through belief and action, the Universe will ultimately do its part.

10. Know your "why" and commit to action consistent with it. Know your strengths and weaknesses. However, always focus on your strengths in order to be better (not perfect), and leverage your weaknesses by finding others who excel where you don't.

Your life is meant to be lived from your true self. Your root cause does not define your true self unless you choose to allow it. As humans, we are conditioned through society to have self-doubt. However, this does not have to be the case. You have the choice to master your Inner Critic, and you deserve that right. Make the commitment today to resolve your root cause and create prosperity. Give the same gift to others by being the example through empowerment once you've mastered your Inner Critic. Self-help through accountability is contagious if done right, and it will make the world a better place—a place flowing with prosperity.

Have Sustainable Prosperity in Your Life

Free guide shows you how to do have the following:

CHRISTOPHER SALEM

➢ Why **your health** and **your wealth factors** have to be in **alignment** to achieve **true prosperity**

➢ How do you **achieve prosperity**

➢ Where do you start with the process to reach **your goals**

Learn the process how to live a truly prosperous life that will have dramatic impact on your health, building wealth, better relationships, and growing your business. Christopher Salem, an advocate for what is right for the people shows the steps necessary to create this for yourself and your family to live in true prosperity.

Access your FREE Guide
"Health + Wealth = Prosperity" at:

www.christophersalem.com/contact/

Lightning Source UK Ltd.
Milton Keynes UK
UKHW021930030620
364324UK00012B/2924